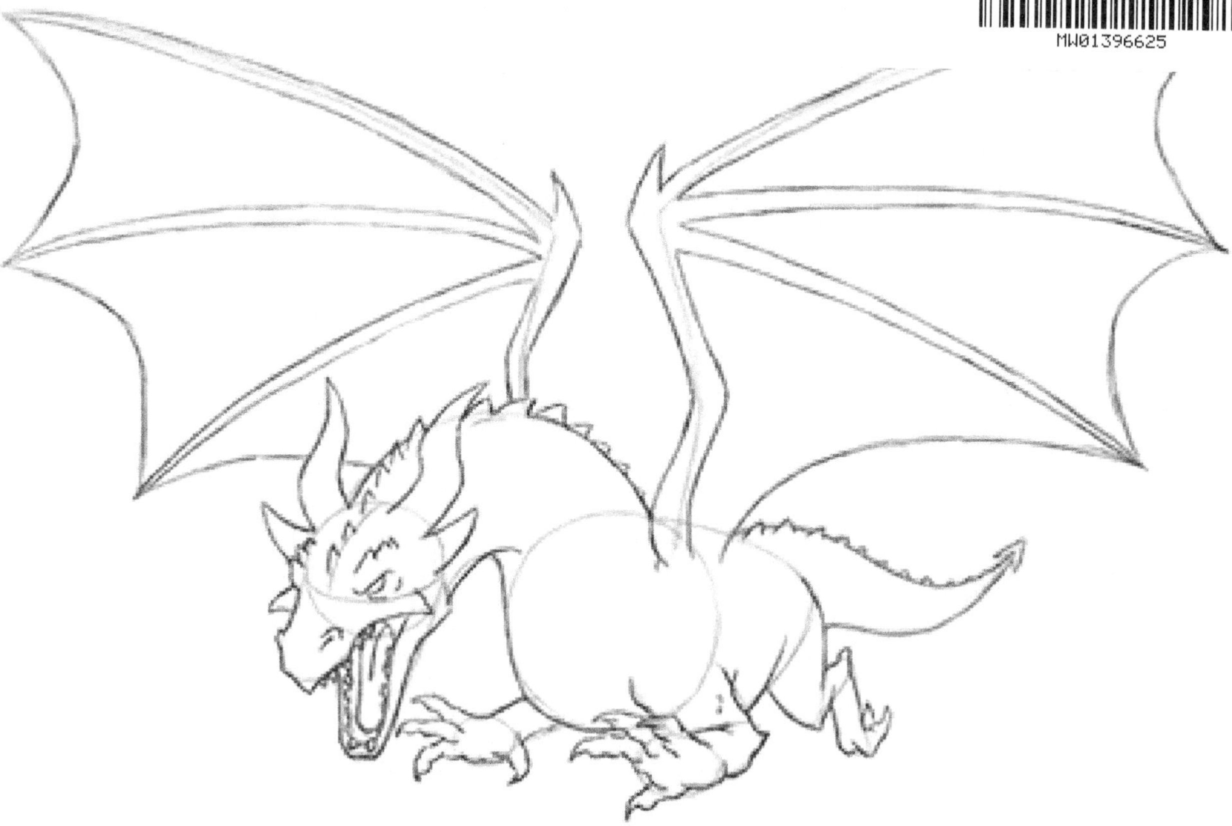

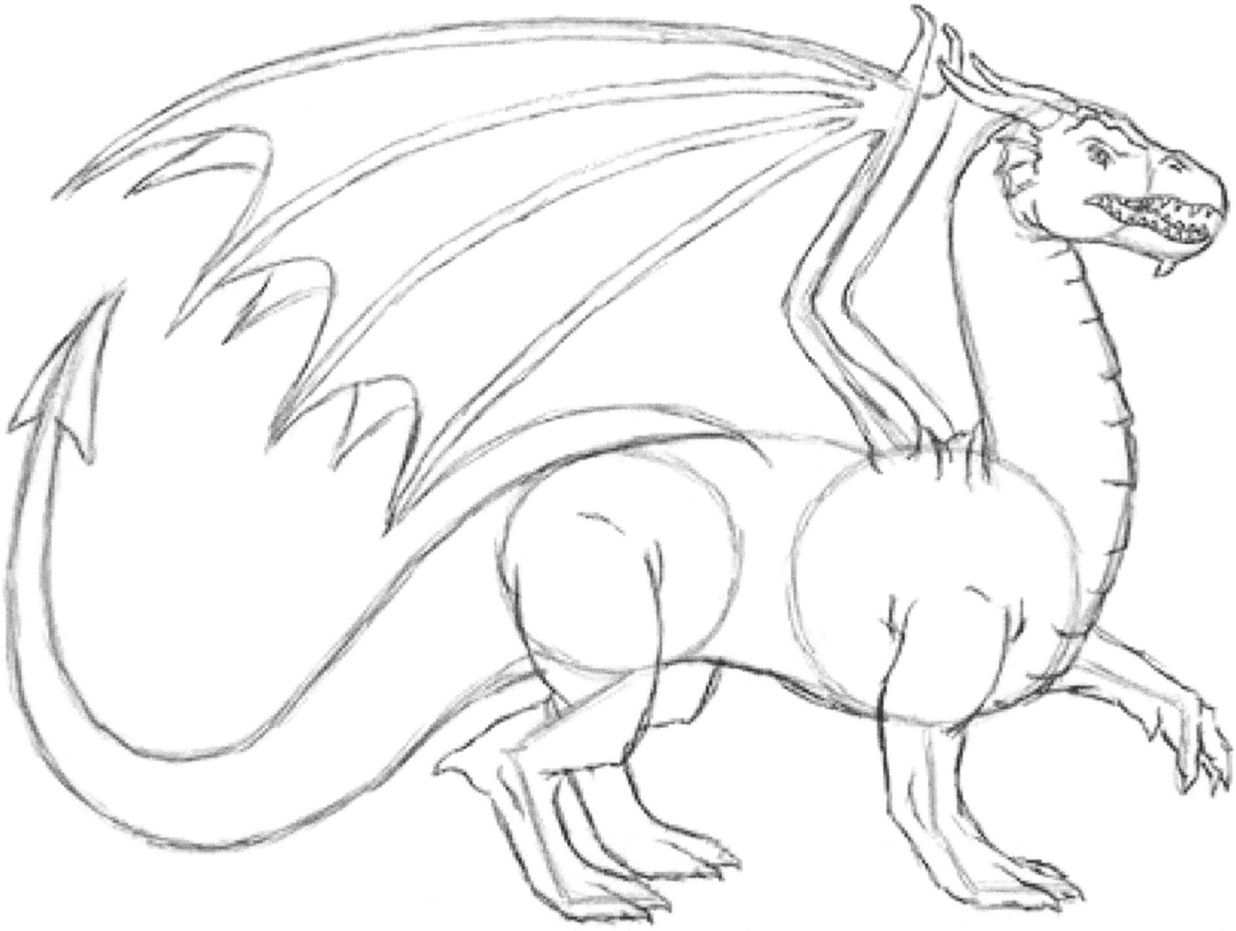

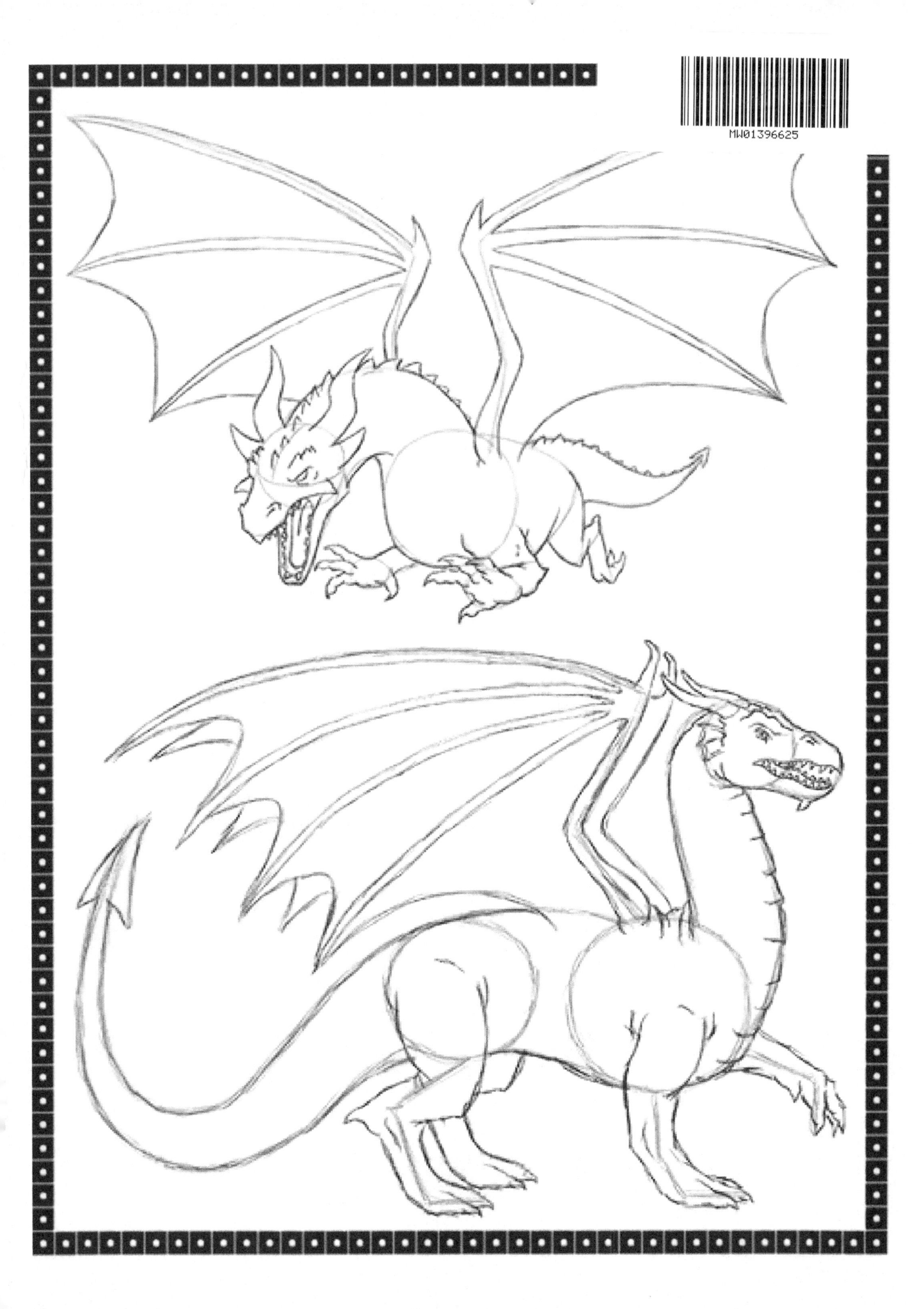

Step 1:
Draw two circles as guides for the dragon's body. They don't have to be perfect. They're just guides. Instead, pay attention to the size and spacing of the circles. That will determine the size of your dragon.

Step 2:
Draw a smaller circle on the upper right side of the dragon's body. The height of the circle will determine the dragon's neck length, so place it accordingly.

Step 3:
Draw an arc next to the head as a guide for the dragon's muzzle.

Step 4:
Draw angled lines below the dragon's body as guides for the legs. If you want your dragon to have longer legs, draw longer lines. Make the squiggles darker in certain areas to create the stripey look.

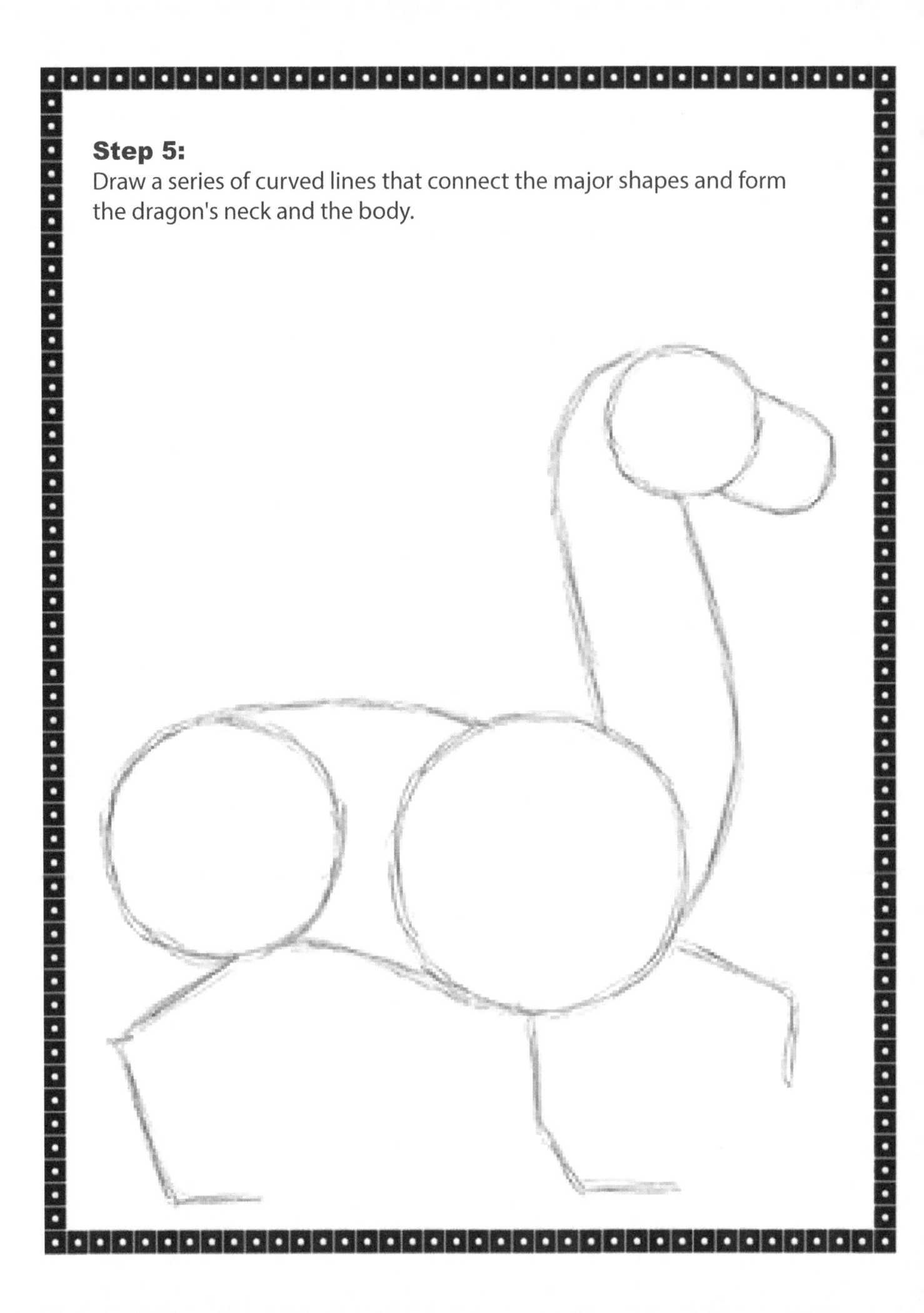

Step 5:
Draw a series of curved lines that connect the major shapes and form the dragon's neck and the body.

Step 6:
Draw a couple of lines that meet at a point on the left side as a guide for the dragon's tail. You can draw the tail as long and curved as you'd like.

Step 7:
Draw an angled line on top of the body as a guide for the dragon's wings. That's it for the initial sketch! From this point, press harder with your pencil to get a more defined sketch.

Step 8:
Draw the dragon's eye on the upper right side inside the circle. The shape of the eye is similar to a football. Shade the inside except for a small circle to represent glare. Draw a few lines surrounding the dragon's eye for extra detail. Above the eye, draw a few jagged lines for a bony structure.

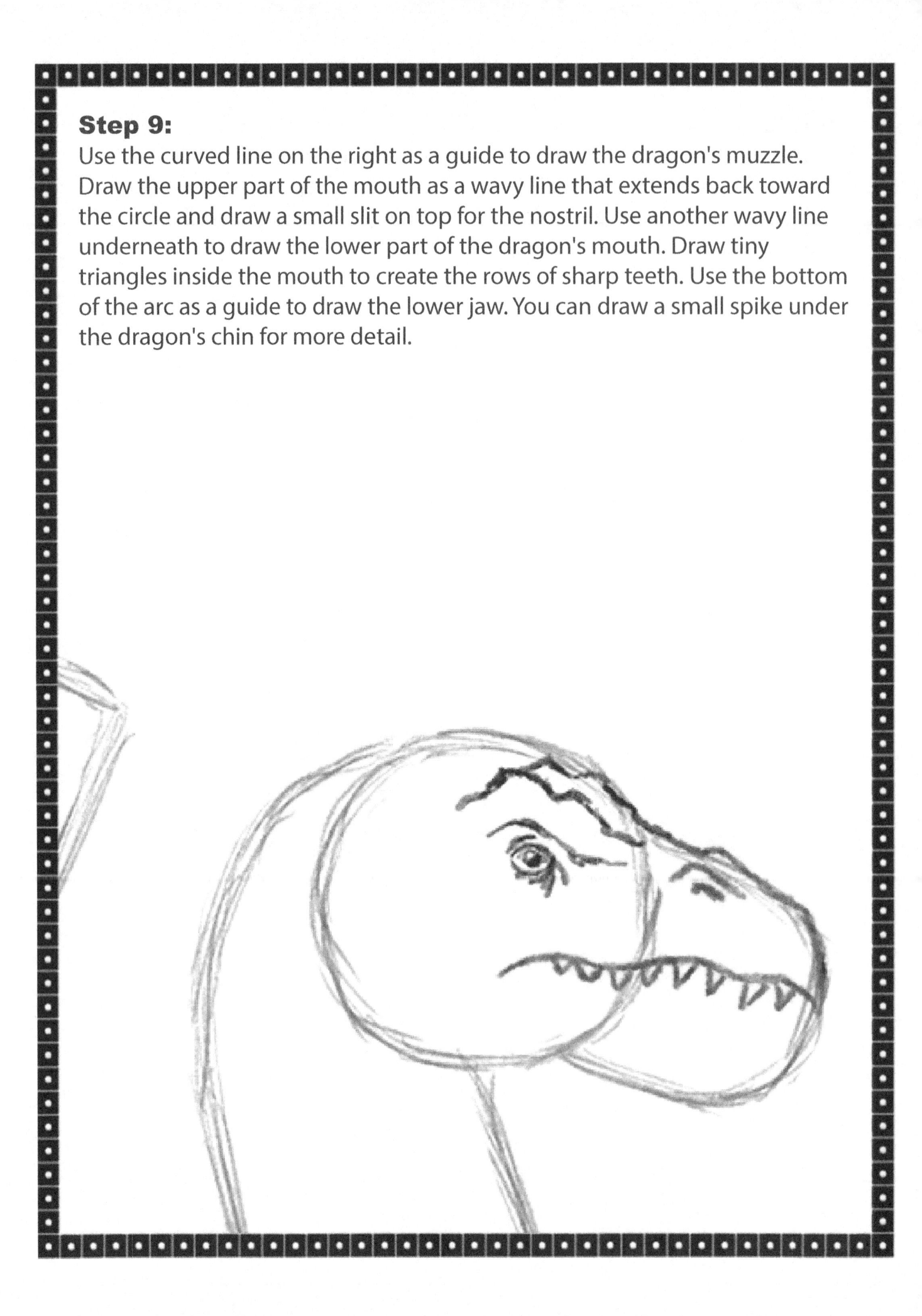

Step 9:
Use the curved line on the right as a guide to draw the dragon's muzzle. Draw the upper part of the mouth as a wavy line that extends back toward the circle and draw a small slit on top for the nostril. Use another wavy line underneath to draw the lower part of the dragon's mouth. Draw tiny triangles inside the mouth to create the rows of sharp teeth. Use the bottom of the arc as a guide to draw the lower jaw. You can draw a small spike under the dragon's chin for more detail.

Step 10:
Draw a series of curved lines on top of the dragon's head for horns. Draw lightly at first to get the structure right, then darken it. Make them longer or shorter, or draw more horns if you'd like.

Step 11:
If you'd like, you can draw an ear below the dragon's horns for more detail.

Step 12:
Using the lines as guides, draw the dragon's hind legs. Draw lightly at first to get the structure right. When you're happy with what you have, go ahead and darken it. Draw a couple of toes at the bottom and a few lines on top to indicate folds of skin. Draw the visible portion of the dragon's leg on the other side.

Step 13:
Use the initial lines as guides to draw the dragon's front legs. Remember to draw lightly at first and only darken once you get the structure right. You can draw the dragon's leg on the other side raised or for a simpler version, draw it next to the other leg like the hind legs. If you draw the leg raised, draw the dragon's toes as a series of angled lines pointing down.

Step 14:
Use the initial angled line as a guide to draw the first part of the dragon's wing. Thicken up the guide line, especially at the base. Draw a pointy spike on the top right angle of the wing as extra detail.

Step 15:
For the second part of the dragon's wing, draw a series of curved, pointy lines inside to give it more structure. Be sure to draw lightly at first to get the structure and spacing of the lines right.

Step 16:
Now that you have the bony structure down, draw a few curved lines in between to get the attached skin that forms the dragon's wing.

Step 17:
Draw the wing on the other side by using the dragon's wing in front as a guide.

Step 18:
Draw the dragon's neck and body using the initial shapes and lines as guides. Use small lines on the right side of the dragon's neck to represent scales.

Step 19:
Darken the shape of the dragon's tail. If you'd like, you can draw an arrow-like point at the end for extra detail.

Step 20 (optional):
For a cleaner look, erase as much as you can of the initial guide lines. Don't worry about erasing all of them. It's okay to leave some behind. Also re-draw any final sketch lines that you may have accidentally erased.

How to Draw a Dragon (Flying)

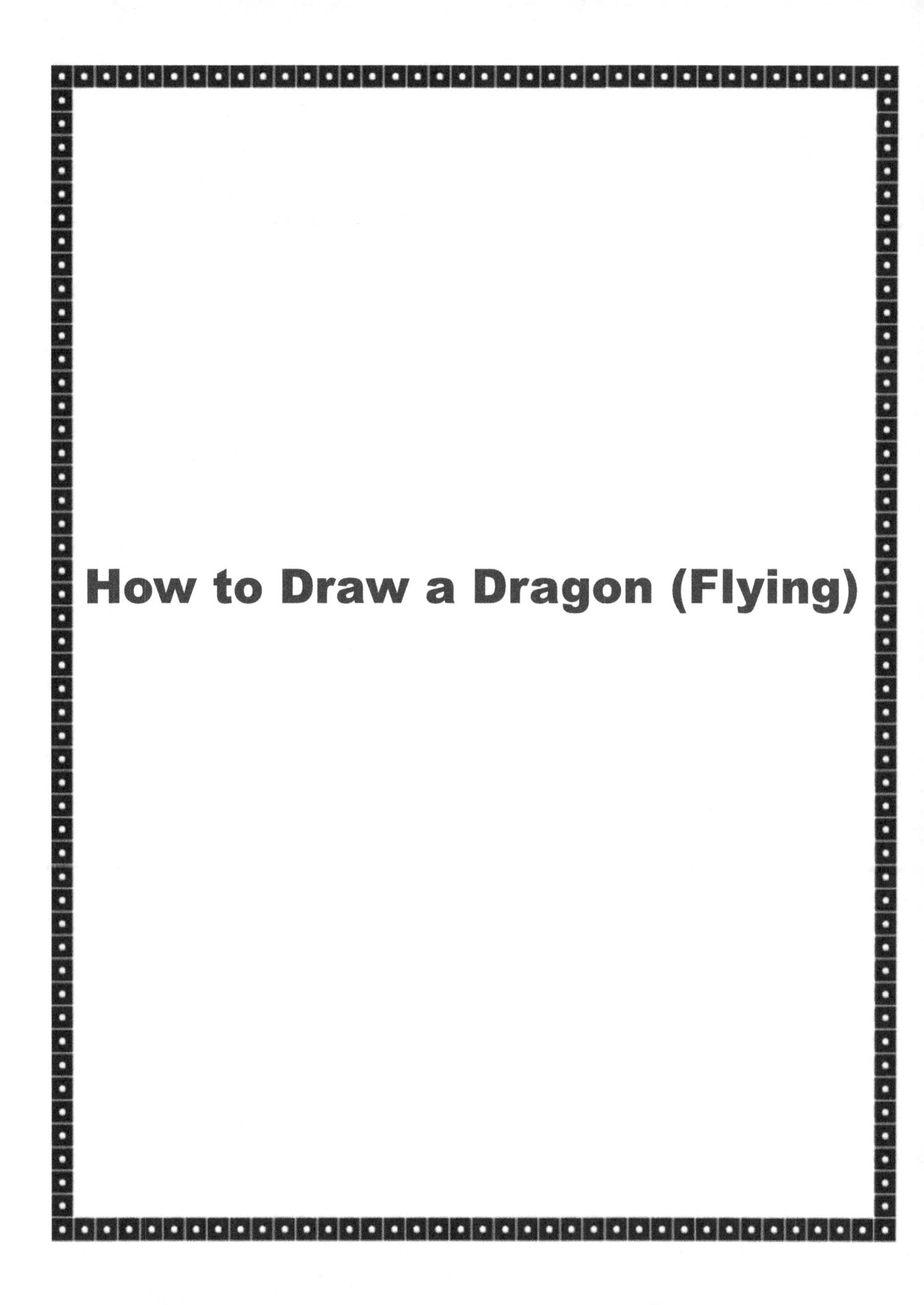

Step 1:
Draw a small circle near the bottom of the paper as a guide for the dragon's body. First make four small marks to indicate the circle's width and height. Then connect the marks using curved lines to form the rest of the circle. If you're struggling drawing the circle, trace the outer rim of a coin, a lid or any other object with a circular edge.

Step 2:
Draw a curved horizontal line across the head. This construction line will help you place the dragon's facial features later. Add a curved vertical line on the top, left side of the head for another construction line.

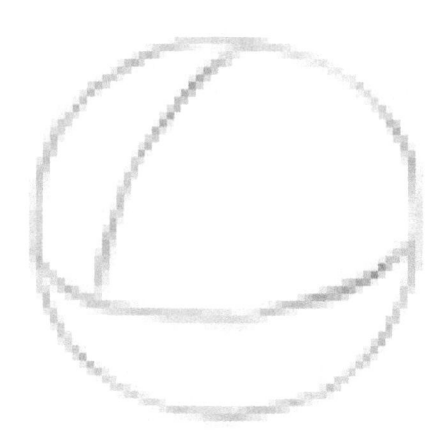

Step 3:
On the lower, left side of the dragon's head, draw a small arc as a guide for the top part of the muzzle. This arc should be similar to the letter U that's slightly tilted to the right.

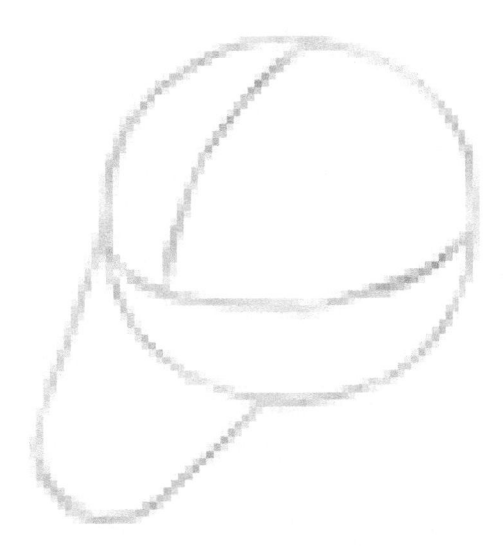

Step 4:
Draw a longer curved line under the head as a guide for the dragon's lower jaw. This guide should be similar to the letter V, but it should have a round bottom instead of pointy.

Step 5:
To the right of the head, draw another circle as a guide for the front part of the dragon's body. Draw this circle the same way as the head. First make four small marks for the width and height, then connect the marks with curved lines. This circle should be about twice the size of the head. Don't draw it too far away from the head, either.

Step 6:
Draw two curved lines that connect the head and the body to form the guide for the dragon's neck. The first line should be long. It should start on the top, left side of the head and end at the top of the body. The line at the bottom should be a lot smaller, and it should go right in the middle of the head and body.

Step 7:
On the lower, right side of the body, draw a small oval as a guide for the first front foot. Add a small arc on the right side of the oval as a guide for the lower half of the leg. On top of the small arc, draw a couple of short lines as guide for the base of the leg. To the left, draw another small oval with a couple of lines that connect to the body as a guide for the dragon's other front leg.

Step 8:
To the right of the big circle, draw a long, curved line as a guide for the back portion of the dragon's body. Don't make this line too wide because the body will be receding in the distance.

Step 9:
On the lower, right side of the dragon's body, draw a small U-shaped line as a guide for the base of the hind leg. To the left, draw a small arc as a guide for the middle section of the hind leg. Below that, draw a long, rectangular shape as a guide for the foot.

Step 10:
On the right side of the body, draw a couple of wavy lines that come to a point as a guide for the dragon's tail. The tail is receding in the distance, so don't draw the guide lines too long.

Step 11:
Above the body, draw two long angled lines as guides for the dragon's wings. Start with a short vertical line. Then angle the line to the left and draw a longer curved horizontal line. Draw the same shape on the right for the other wing, but this time point the end toward the right. Dragons are mythical creatures, so you can make the wings as long or as short as you'd like. That's it for the initial sketch! From this point on, press harder with your pencil to get a more defined sketch.

Step 12:
Inside the dragon's head, draw a small angled line similar to a check mark for the lower part of the brow. Use the construction lines as guides for the brow's placement. Draw a curved line underneath for the eye. Add a couple of lines below to emphasize the rough skin. Above the eye, draw three small spikes for the top part of the bony brow. On the left side of the circle, draw three more spikes for the brow that's on the other side of the head.

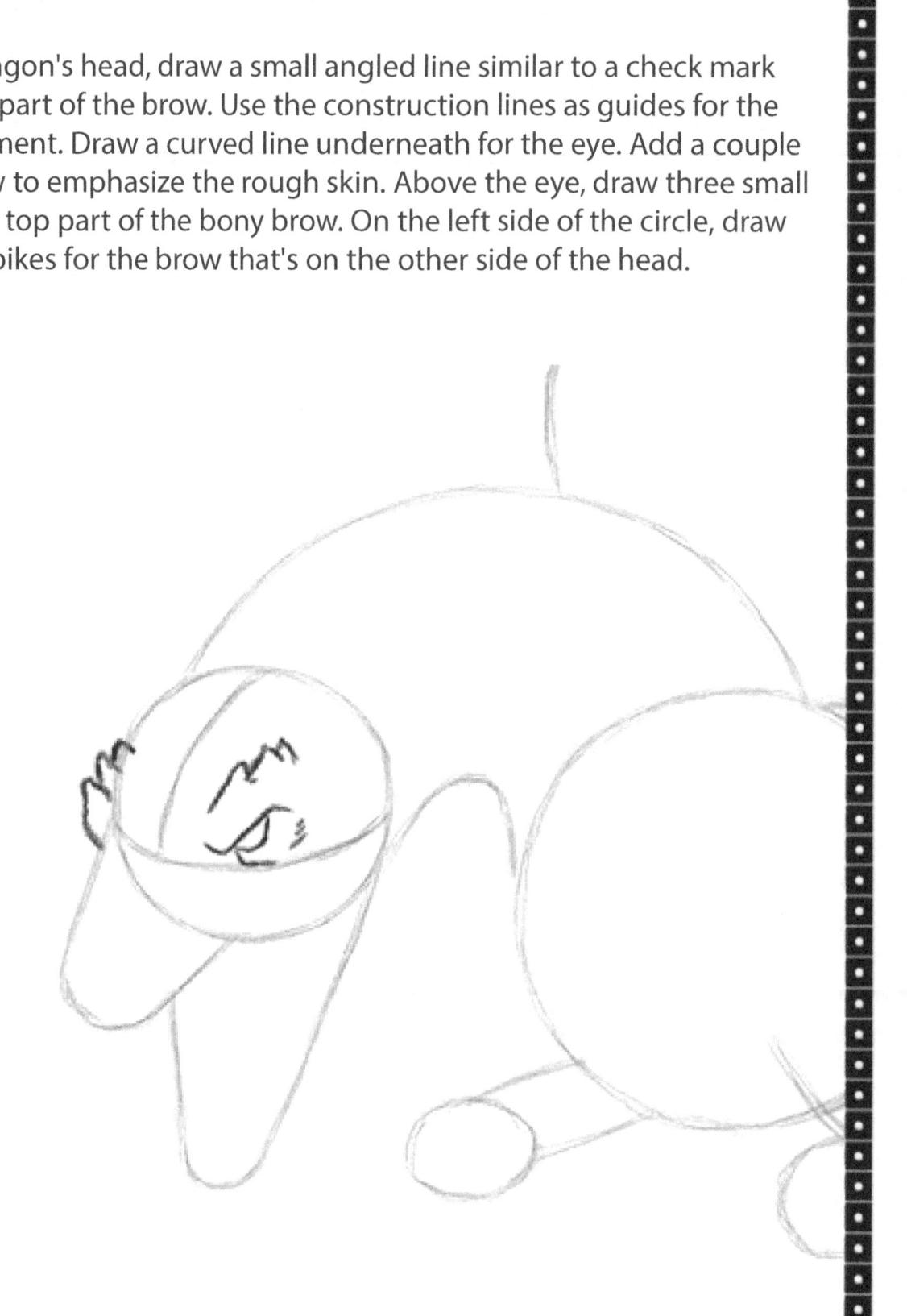

Step 13:
Use the curved line on the lower, left side as a guide to draw the top part of the dragon's muzzle. Darken the path of the guide and give it an extra bump on the side for the nostril and a spike at the bottom for the mouth. Continue following the path of the guide but draw a spike on the right side of the jaw, right below the eye. Near the tip of the dragon's muzzle, draw a small slit with a curved line on top for the other nostril.

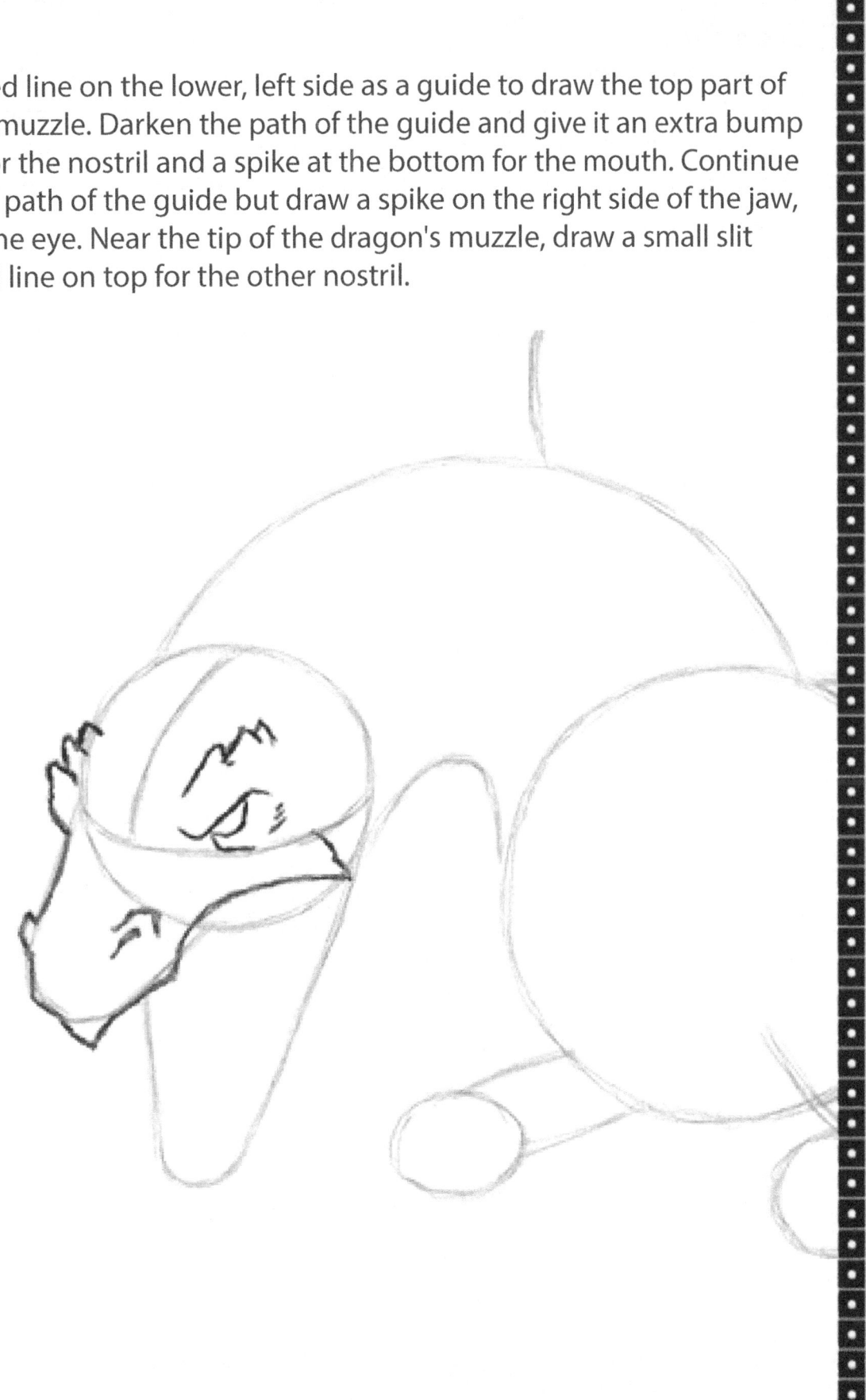

Step 14:
On the other side of the head, draw a triangle- like shape for the other jaw spike. Draw a series of small V-shaped lines along the lower edge of the muzzle for this fire-breathing dragon's teeth. Darken the guide below to create the shape of the jaw. Add an extra curve to the line at the top for the powerful jaw muscles.

Step 15:
Draw the inside of the open mouth by first drawing a long line on the right side. Add a few jagged, pointy shapes at the bottom and on the left side for the dragon's teeth. Add a small line on the top, right for the piece of skin that connects the jaw.

Step 16:
Inside the mouth, draw a few more jagged shapes on the right side for the teeth. Near the middle, draw a couple of curved lines for the dragon's tongue.

Step 17:
On either side of the dragon's head, draw a spike using a couple of curved lines that come to a point. You can make these horns bigger, smaller or exclude them altogether!

Step 18:
On top of the head, draw two horns using a couple of wavy lines that come to a point. Sketch lightly at first. When you get the shape of the dragon's horns right, darken the lines. The base of the horns should be thick, and they should gradually come to a point at the top. You can give your dragon more horns or change it any way you want. These steps are more like guide lines.

Step 19:
Draw a series of triangle-like shapes across the forehead and neck for more spikes. Darken the initial curved lines to create the shape of the dragon's neck.

Step 20:
Draw a series of small, triangle-like shapes along the top edge of the neck for more spikes. The body will be receding because of the perspective, so make the spikes smaller the farther back they are. Darken the left edge of the guides under the neck to create the shape of the dragon's chest.

Step 21:
Use the shapes under the dragon's body as guides to draw the first front leg. On the top, left side of the initial oval, draw a couple of short lines that come to a point for the first digit. To the right, draw another digit using a couple more curved lines. Add a third digit farther right the same way. Make sure you make them pointy at the end for the claws. Darken the bottom section of the initial circle and add a thumb- like digit on the lower left side. Darken the outer edges of the initial guides to finish the shape of the leg. Add a small spike to the elbow.

Step 22:
Use the shapes on the left side of the body as guides to draw the other front leg the same way. First draw the three digits on top of the initial oval using short, curved lines. Then darken the outer edges of the initial guides to finish the leg's shape. Add the dragon's thumb on the lower, right side.

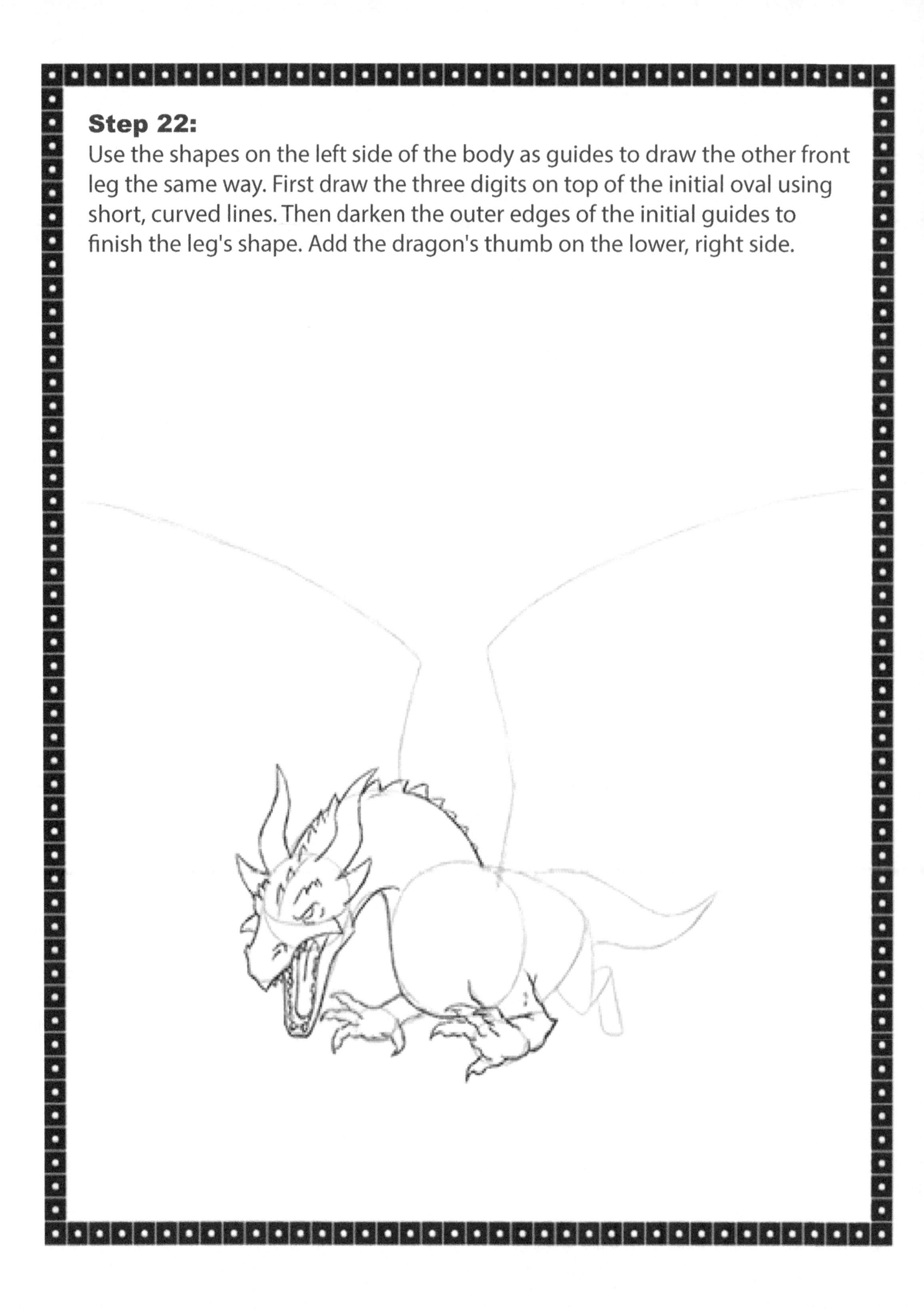

Step 23:
Use the lines on the lower, right side of the body as guide to draw the dragon's hind leg. Simply darken the outer edges of the initial guides to create the shape of the leg. Use a couple of short lines that curve to the right at the bottom of the foot for the digits.

Step 24:
Use the long, curved lines above the body as guides to draw the first part of this fire-breathing dragon's wings. Follow the basic path of the guide as you make the first section of the wing thicker. Add a small spike where the line bends, then thicken up the curved left side too. Make the tip pointy on the left side and leave a gap where the shape bends on the inside. Now use the line on the right as a guide to draw the first part of that wing the same way. You can bend the lower section of the wing more. Add a spike where the wing bends at the top too. Make the right tip pointy. You can draw the dragon's wings a lot bigger if you'd like (and if you have enough room!)

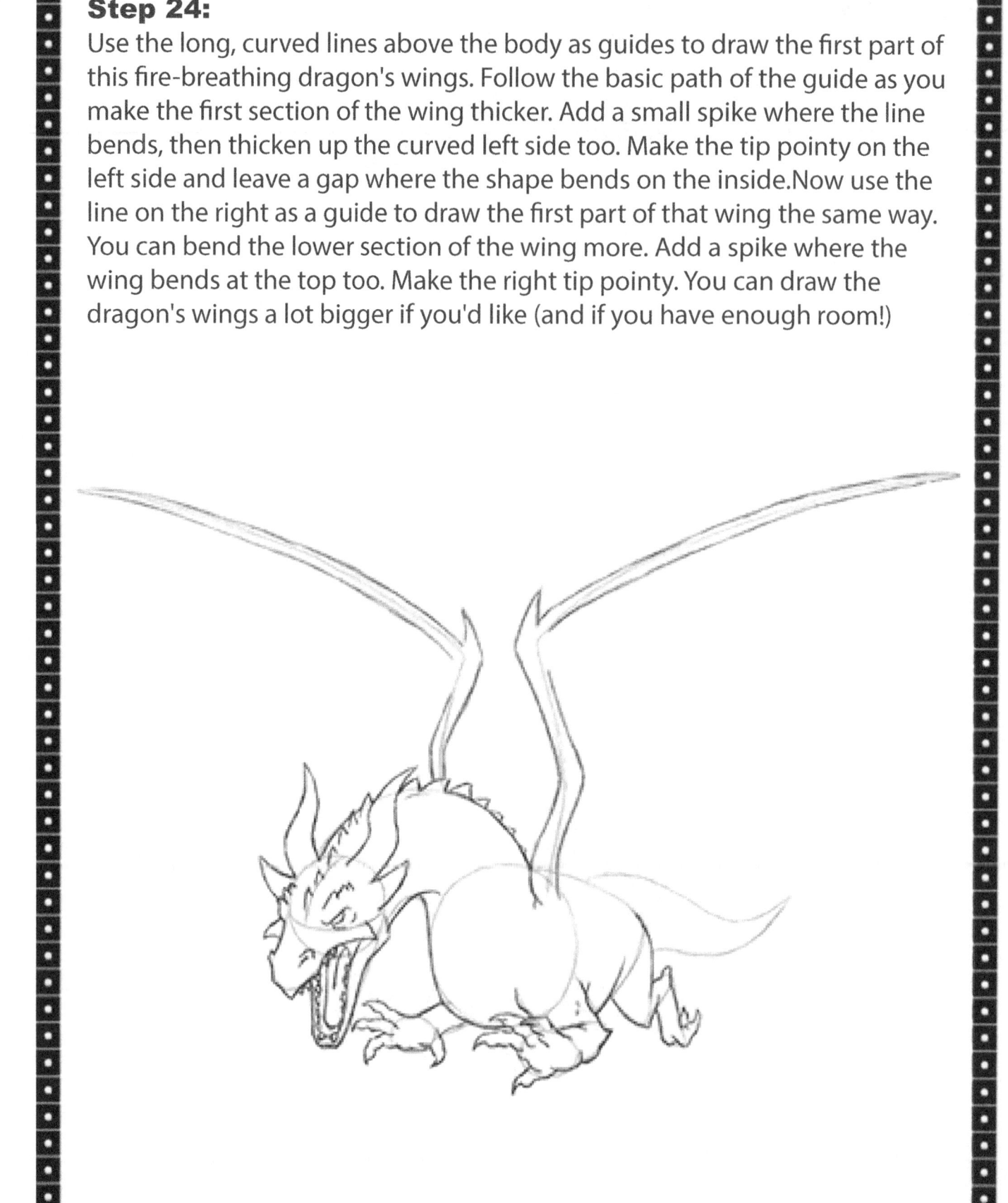

Step 25:
Draw a couple more long, thin, curved shapes where the sections bend for the second part of the wings. These are the segments that are going to hold the skin that makes up the dragon's wings. The lowest segment should have more of a diagonal orientation. They should all be pointy at the end. Draw two more of these segments pointing in the opposite direction on the right side for the other wing. Draw lightly at first so that it's easy to erase if you make a mistake. Darken the lines only when you get the shape right.

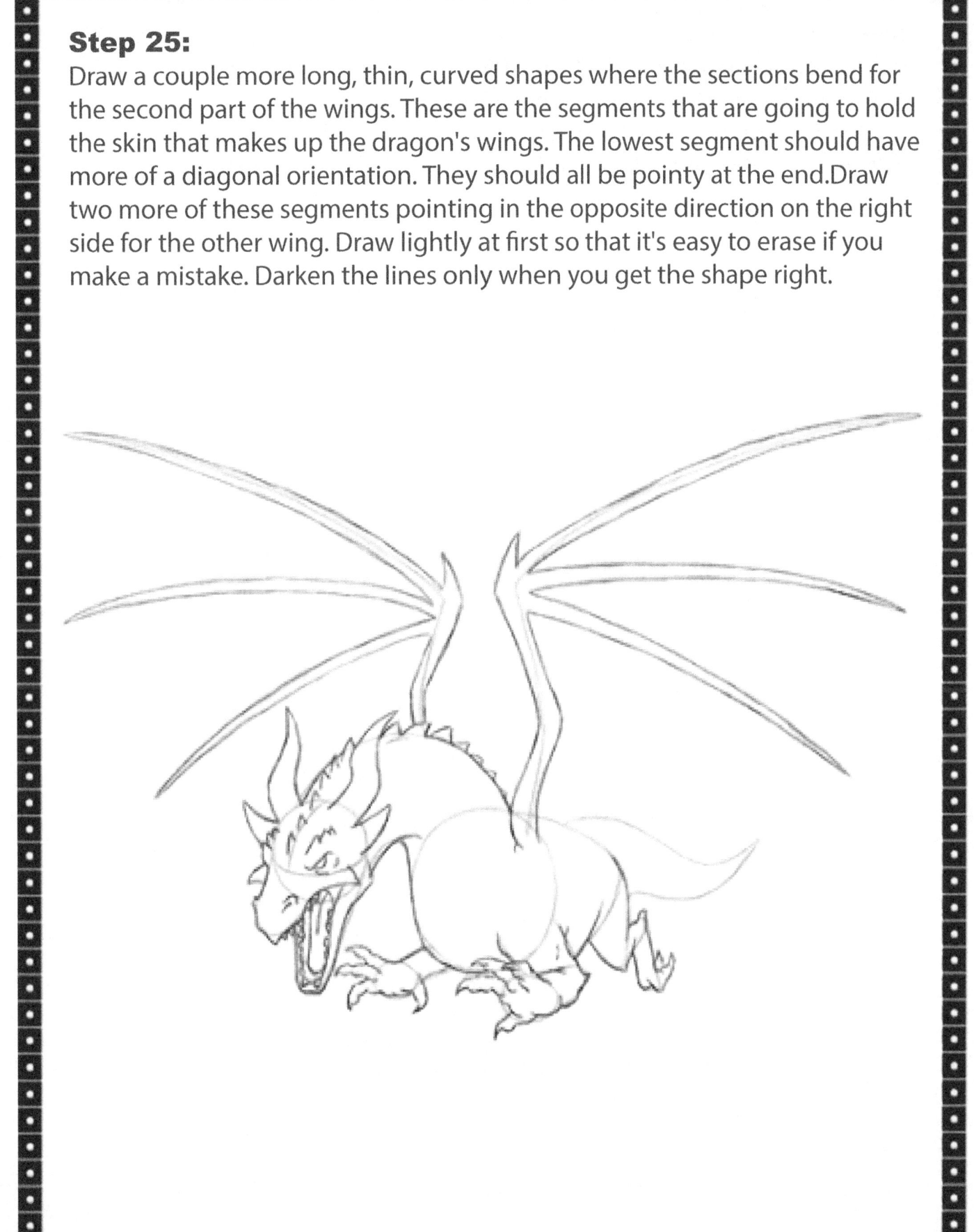

Step 26:
Draw a curved line that connects each of the thin, long segments to finish the dragon's wings. The curved line at the bottom should have more of a horizontal orientation. Don't overlap the head. Draw the lines on the right too. The line at the bottom should be long , and it should connect to the body.

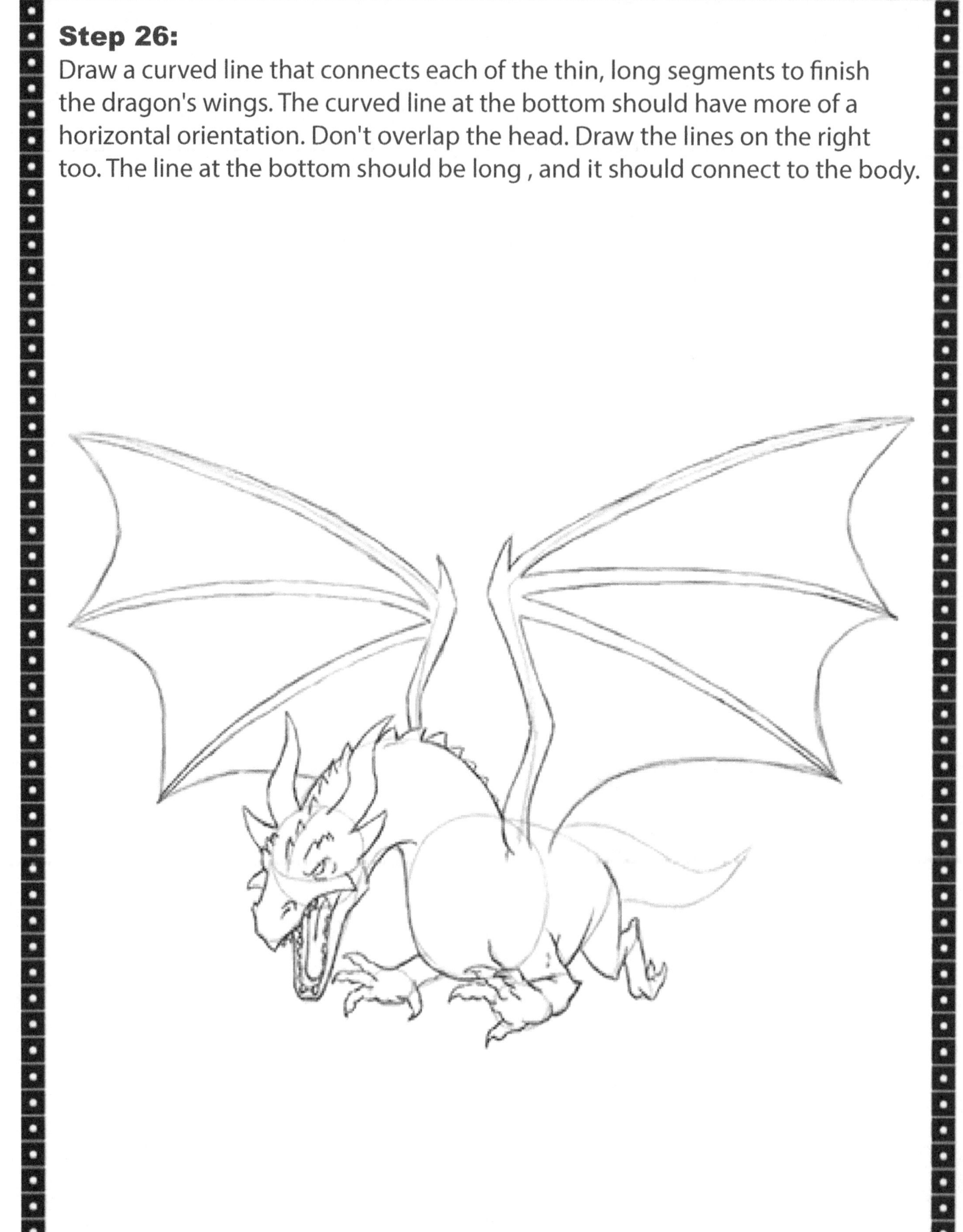

Step 27:
Darken the wavy lines on the right side to create the shape of the dragon's tail. Draw a series of triangle-like shapes that gradually get smaller along the top edge of the tail for spikes. Draw another triangle-like shape at the end for the arrow-like tip of the tail.

Step 28:
For a cleaner look, erase as much as you can of the initial guide lines. Don't worry about erasing all of the guides. It's okay to leave some behind. Re-draw any final sketch lines you may have accidentally erased.

Final Step:
Add some shading to your dragon drawing to give it more dimension and volume. Pick the direction of the light source when shading so that the shadows are consistent with it. We're going to be adding flames to the mouth later, so in this case, the shadows will mainly be on the right, away from the mouth. Vary the pressure on your pencil to get different degrees of tonal value. You can add even more value throughout your fire-breathing dragon drawing for extra detail. Use a series of tiny, squiggly lines all over the body to represent the skin's rough, scaly texture. Use horizontal lines on the chest. Don't overthink the squiggly lines. Just add them randomly all over the body to create texture. Because dragons are mythical creatures, you can shade yours any way you want.
You can add stripes, spots or even color it!

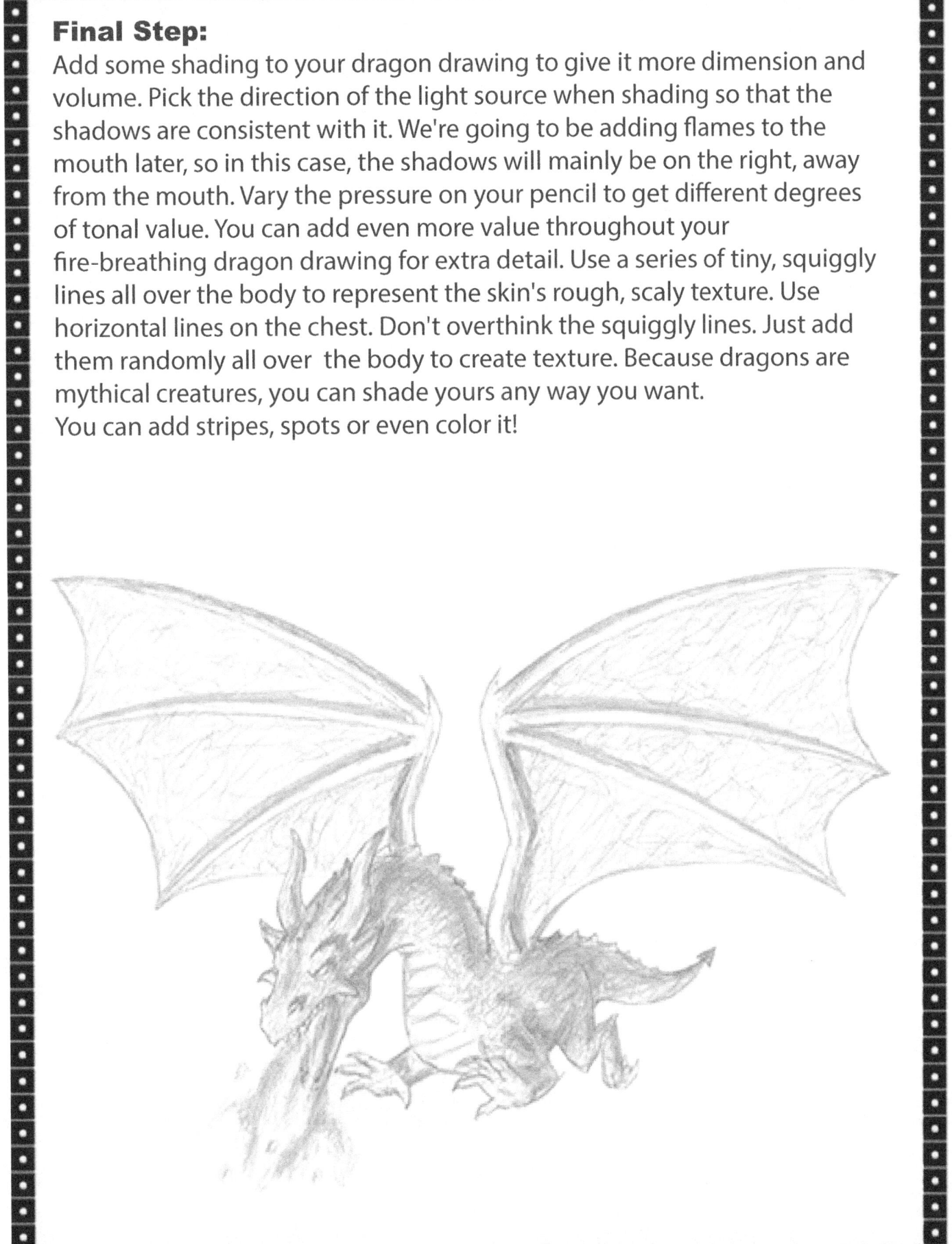

Made in the USA
Las Vegas, NV
11 October 2023